# UNCOVERING THE PAST:
## ANALYZING PRIMARY SOURCES

# CIVIL RIGHTS

# HILARIE STATON

Crabtree Publishing Company
www.crabtreebooks.com

**Author:** Hilarie Staton
**Publishing plan research and development:** Reagan Miller
**Editor-in-Chief:** Lionel Bender
**Editors:** Simon Adams, Anastasia Suen
**Proofreaders:** Laura Booth, Wendy Scavuzzo
**Project coordinator:** Kelly Spence
**Design and photo research:** Ben White
**Production:** Kim Richardson
**Production coordinator and prepress technician:** Ken Wright
**Print coordinator:** Margaret Amy Salter

**Consultant:** Amie Wright,
The New York Public Library

This book was produced for
Crabtree Publishing Company by
Bender Richardson White

**Library and Archives Canada Cataloguing in Publication**

Staton, Hilarie N., author
    Civil rights / Hilarie Staton.

(Uncovering the past: analyzing primary sources)
Includes index.
Issued in print and electronic formats.
ISBN 978-0-7787-1549-8 (bound).--ISBN 978-0-7787-1553-5 (pbk.).--ISBN 978-1-4271-1601-7 (pdf).--ISBN 978-1-4271-1597-3 (html)

    1. Civil rights movements--United States--History--20th century--Juvenile literature. 2. African Americans--Civil rights--History--20th century--Juvenile literature. I. Title.

E185.61.S73 2015          j940.53'11          C2014-908081-6
                                              C2014-908082-4

**Library of Congress Cataloging-in-Publication Data**

Staton, Hilarie N.
  Civil rights / Hilarie Staton.
    pages cm. -- (Uncovering the past: analyzing primary sources)
  Includes index.
  ISBN 978-0-7787-1549-8 (reinforced library binding) -- ISBN 978-0-7787-1553-5 (pbk.) -- ISBN 978-1-4271-1601-7 (pdf) -- ISBN 978-1-4271-1597-3 (html)
  1. African Americans--Civil rights--History--Juvenile literature. 2. Civil rights movements--United States--History--20th century--Juvenile literature. 3. United States--Race relations--Juvenile literature. I. Title.

  E185.61.S794 2015
  323.1196'073--dc23
                                              2014046553

## Crabtree Publishing Company

Printed in Canada/022015/MA20150101

www.crabtreebooks.com          1-800-387-7650

**Published in Canada**
**Crabtree Publishing**
616 Welland Ave.
St. Catharines, ON
L2M 5V6

**Published in the United States**
**Crabtree Publishing**
PMB 59051
350 Fifth Avenue, 59th Floor
New York, NY 10118

**Published in the United Kingdom**
**Crabtree Publishing**
Maritime House
Basin Road North, Hove
BN41 1WR

**Published in Australia**
**Crabtree Publishing**
3 Charles Street
Coburg North
VIC, 3058

# UNCOVERING THE PAST
## ANALYZING PRIMARY SOURCES

# REMEMBERING THE PAST

*"We are not makers of history. We are made by history."*

Dr. Martin Luther King, Jr.

Do you remember something that happened to you last year? Do family pictures help you remember some special time years ago? Maybe it was a family trip or a birthday party. The other people who were there may have a different idea of what happened that day. These memories are part of who you are. It is *your* **history**.

Our country's history is made from memories, too. **Historians** search for these memories. They ask questions about life and events. They keep looking for information to understand what happened. Sometimes it is easy to find this information because they have many **sources**. It is much harder to find out exactly what happened centuries ago because there are fewer sources. Historians use many sources to build a picture of the past.

This book is about uncovering memories of the **civil rights movement** in the United States. It took place during the 1950s and 1960s. Because it wasn't very long ago, there are many sources.

## DEFINITIONS

Historians use special words to talk about time:

**Decade:** A period of 10 years
**Century:** A period of 100 years
**Era:** A period during which something, an event, or a person is very important. It describes a time period, not a set number of years. This book is about the civil rights era.
**Generation:** Refers to a group of people who were born around the same time; parents are considered to be a separate generation from their children.

WE DEMAND EQUAL RIGHTS NOW!

WE MARCH FOR INTEGRATED SCHOOLS NOW! RIGHTS NOW!

WE DEMAND AN END POLICE BRUTALITY NOW!

DEMAND DECENT HOUSING NOW!

DE AN TO N

JOBS and FREEDOM

▲ The March on Washington, D.C., was held on August 28, 1963. About 250,000 people marched into the city to ask the United States **Congress** to pass a civil rights **bill**.

## THE CIVIL RIGHTS MOVEMENT

The civil rights era was from about 1954 until about 1971. During it, many people fought for **African Americans** to have the same **civil rights** as white Americans. Civil rights are the rights and protections the government promises all people. In the United States, they include freedom of speech, the right to be treated the same as others in public places, and the right to vote. People also wanted to end **racism**. This is a belief that one **race** is not as good as another.

The U.S. **constitution** grants the same civil rights to every person. The laws in some southern states took these rights away from African Americans. They were **discriminated** against because they were not white.

▼ In September 1962, President Kennedy sent troops to The University of Mississippi. Whites were **rioting** because a **federal court** ruled that James Meredith must be allowed to become its first African-American student.

### DEFINITIONS

What we call people changes. The words that everyone used in the past may be an insult today. Here are a few terms used for the people whose ancestors came to America from Africa:

**African American:** The modern, most acceptable term for people in the United States with dark skin whose ancestors came from Africa

**Black:** A common term used for people who have dark skin

**Negro:** The most common polite term until the late 1960s. Today, it is considered rude unless it is used in something written in the past

**Colored:** A term for people who have dark skin. It is no longer considered acceptable in the United States

Other more racist words were used. Some people in the South used them without thinking. Others screamed them as an insult.

*". . . no school in our state will be integrated while I am your Governor. I shall do everything in my power to prevent integration in our schools."*

Governor of Mississippi, Ross Barnett, September 13, 1962, disagreeing with the federal court's ruling

**Discrimination** is when a person's civil rights are interfered with just because of one thing such as their race. During the civil rights movement, people held a series of organized events to get equal treatment and protection for African Americans.

But every **movement** has two sides. Some white Americans, especially in the South, were violently against these changes. Because of these differences, people on both sides went to court, marched, voted, and rioted.

Historians of the civil rights era tell the story of a movement that changed the United States.

▼ This campaign button for Barack Obama tells that it was used in 08 (2008) when he ran for office with Joe Biden. That year, he became the first African American to run for president and win. He became a symbol of how the civil rights movement had changed the United States.

# TYPES OF EVIDENCE

*"Once I got to the Mall and the Reflecting Pool, I saw this mass of humanity—people from all of these different towns, especially from the South."*

Nan Grogan Orrock, who attended the March on Washington, D.C.

Historians use many sources to learn about the past. A source is any place you get information. It could be a picture, a person, a book, or a law.

The details of history's memories are found in primary sources. Primary sources are anything that was created or used by someone who was there. Primary sources give historians the **evidence**, or facts, that prove what happened. They use these facts to form their ideas. They learn something a little different from each source. They put them together to form a picture of an era, an event, or a person. They use many primary sources to help them understand the whole picture.

The civil rights movement took place only a few decades ago, so many primary sources exist. These include photographs and recordings of speeches and news shows. Many letters, newspaper articles, and government **documents** exist from that time. Even the songs people sang are a primary source.

▶ Civil rights leaders, including Dr. Martin Luther King, Jr., A. Philip Randolph, and Roy Wilkins lead the 1963 March on Washington.

## TYPES OF PRIMARY SOURCES

Some primary sources are:

- Photographs taken at an event
- Interviews, diaries, or letters from people who were there
- Newspaper articles written during that time
- Government documents from that time
- Physical objects from that time
- Audio or news footage taken at that time
- Lyrics to songs sung at that time

## SECONDARY SOURCES

Some sources are **secondary sources**. A secondary source is based on facts from many primary sources. They are not based on the writer being there.

History writers gather facts from many primary sources. They ask questions about the era and search for the answers in primary sources. Then they **analyze** their evidence. They draw conclusions and form opinions about the people, time, and place. They write a secondary source with their ideas. That secondary source can be written anytime after an event. It could be from one day to hundreds of years later.

Different writers choose different sources. They might draw different conclusions because they find different evidence. Which sources they choose might determine how well they can support their ideas. That's why history is like memories—everyone remembers things a little differently.

▶ Alex Haley wrote the popular book *Roots*. He used historic events to create his story. Some people thought the book was nonfiction, or true. When they found out it wasn't, they felt tricked. Others found mistakes in it. It is not a secondary source, but a combination of fiction and nonfiction.

## TYPES OF SECONDARY SOURCES

Some secondary sources are:

- Encyclopedias filled with short articles on many different topics
- Textbooks used to teach a subject
- Newspaper or magazine articles written about a past event
- Interviews with experts who did not participate in the event
- TV shows about the history of an event or a time in the past

Some secondary sources are history books about a whole era. In his books about the civil rights era, such as *Parting the Waters: America in the King Years 1954–63*, Taylor Branch used various primary sources. He searched for new evidence. He interviewed people and uncovered government files.

In her book, *Freedom Summer: The 1964 Struggle for Civil Rights in Mississippi*, Susan Goldman Rubin used many different types of primary sources. On page seven, she drew the conclusion: "The week of training attracted **national** attention. . . ." She knew this because of primary sources. She was not there, but she talked to people who were. She also read articles in national magazines by people who were there.

Sometimes writers do not use primary sources. They read only secondary sources. These writers base their conclusions on the conclusions of others. Most are careful to choose writers who have used primary sources to provide strong evidence for their ideas.

▲ In this 1967 fictional movie, African-American actor Sidney Poitier's character must deal with racism and **injustice** in the South. Poitier was the first African American to receive an Academy Award for a leading role. The country's focus on civil rights changed how Hollywood saw African-American actors and allowed them to get better roles than before.

*"Historians have also criticized the emphasis on King and other individual civil rights leaders. Too much attention has been given, they argue, to ministers and national leaders at the expense of local people."*

Anthony J. Badger, historian

# INTERPRETATION

*"The 'separate but equal' doctrine adopted in Plessy v. Ferguson, [in 1896] . . . has no place in the field of public education."*

From *Brown v. Board of Education*,
Supreme Court of the United States, May 17, 1954

Historians are like detectives. They read **text sources**—anything with words—very carefully. They ask questions and search for answers.

They analyze the text to learn about the **context,** or setting. The context is everything about a time and place, including what life was like, events, and people's ideas. During the civil rights era, articles written in New York had a different context from those written in Mississippi. The laws and ideas were different in each place. The context of the writers and their readers were different. When we read it now, we must understand the context to understand the material.

Context can also help understand **bias.** Bias is an opinion in favor of or against something. A strong bias may reveal a **prejudice**—an opinion that is unbalanced or unfair. Prejudices are not based on real information. During the civil rights era, many sources showed strong prejudices. The two pictures on pages 14 and 15 show two different biases, but which one shows strong prejudices?

Historians search for evidence to support their main ideas, to make the context clear, and to reveal the author's bias. They put the facts together in **chronological** order, or the sequence in which they happened. They analyze events to find what caused it or what happened as a result of it.

▶ **The New York Times** is a nationally important newspaper. On Tuesday, May 18, 1954, its main story was about the United States **Supreme Court's** decision, *Brown v. Board of Education.*

"All the News
That's Fit to Print"

VOL. CIII ... No. 35,178.

## HIGH CO
## 9-TO-0 L

### McCarthy H

SENATOR IS IRATE Commun

By Vesse

President Orders Aides
Not to Disclose Details
of Top-Level Meeting

State Departmen
News Gravely B
of Red Infiltra

*President's letter and excerpts
from transcript, Pages 24, 25, 26.*

By W. H. LAWRENCE
Special to The New York Times.

WASHINGTON, May 17—A secrecy directive by President Eisenhower resulted today in an abrupt recess for at least a week of the Senate's Army-McCarthy hearings.

Democratic and Republican Senators, some publicly and some privately, predicted that the investigation might never resume in earnest. However, there were other Senators who insisted that the investigation would go on to completion.

The recess was voted after Herbert Brownell Jr., the Attorney General, disclosed formally that criminal prosecutions might be instituted against those in-

Special to The New York Times

WASHINGTON, May State Department said it had reliable informa... "an important shipment had been sent from Co... controlled territory to G... It said the arms, ne... unloaded at Puerto Barr... temala, had been shipp... Stettin, a former Germ... seaport, which has been ... by Communist Poland sin... War II. The Guatemalan ... has been frequently acc... being influenced by Com...

"Because of the origin ... arms, the point of their er... tion, their destination a...

SOVIET BIDS VIE
CEASE ANTIRIG

**ANALYZE THIS**

This newspaper was from what city? Is this city in the South? Does this seem to be a news article or an opinion piece? Does this seem to be an important event? How do you know?

# The New York Times.

Copyright, 1954, by The New York Times Company.

NEW YORK, TUESDAY, MAY 18, 1954.

Times Square, New York 36, N. Y.
Telephone LAckawanna 4-1000

**LATE CITY EDITION**
Fair and cool today. Mostly sunny, continued cool tomorrow.
Temperature Range Today—Max., 68; Min., 52
Temperature Yesterday—Max., 69; Min., 61
Full U. S. Weather Bureau Report, Page 31

FIVE CENTS

## ...T BANS SCHOOL SEGREGATION; ...ISION GRANTS TIME TO COMPLY

### ...ring Off a Week as Eisenhower Bars Report

### ...as Unloaded in Guatemala ...Polish Port, U. S. Learns

**Embassy Says Nation of Central America May Buy Munitions Anywhere**

Barrios last Saturday, the State Department reported, carrying a large shipment of armament consigned to the Guatemalan Government.

The State Department did not divulge the exact quantity of the arms, their nature or where they had been manufactured.

Reliable sources told The New York Times, however, that ten freight car loads of goods listed in the manifest as "hardware" had been unloaded from this ship and sent to the city of Guatemala since Sunday. Guatemala is 150 miles from Puerto Barrios. The

Continued on Page 10, Column 5

...ork Times      May 18, 1954
...arms arrival (cross)

Of arms, involved, the ...nt of State considers ...is a development of ...the announcement said. ...ter arrived at Puerto

### ...olleges' Board ...Pick Chairman

...rd of Higher Educa-...unable to elect a ...its annual meeting ...at Hunter College. ...man said it was the ...within memory of ...cials" that such a

## 2 TAX PROJECTS DIE IN ESTIMATE BOARD

Beer Levy and More Parking Collections Killed—Payroll

### REACTION OF SOUTH

**'Breathing Spell' for Adjustment Tempers Region's Feelings**

By JOHN N. POPHAM
Special to The New York Times.

CHATTANOOGA, Tenn., May 17—The South's reaction to the Supreme Court's decision outlawing racial segregation in public schools appeared to be tempered considerably today.

The time lag allowed for carrying out the required transitions seemed to be the major factor in that reaction.

Southern leaders of both races in political, educational and community service fields expressed comment that covered a wide range. Some spoke bitter words that verged on defiance. Others ranged from sharp disagreement to predictions of peaceful and successful adjustment in accord with the ruling.

But underneath the surface of much of the comment, it was evident that many Southerners recognized that the decision had laid down the legal principle rejecting segregation in public education facilities.

They also noted that it had left

**LEADERS IN SEGREGATION FIGHT:** Lawyers who led battle before U. S. Supreme Court for abolition of segregation in public schools congratulate one another as they leave court after announcement of decision. Left to right: George E. C. Hayes, Thurgood Marshall and James M. Nabrit.

Associated Press Wirephoto

## MORETTIS' LAWYER MUST BARE TALKS

Jersey Court Orders Counsel to Racketeers in Bergen to Divulge Data to Grand Jury

## RULING TO FIGURE IN '54 CAMPAIGN

Decision Tied to Eisenhower —Russell Leads Southerners in Criticism of Court

### 1896 RULING UPSET

**'Separate but Equal' Doctrine Held Out of Place in Education**

*Text of Supreme Court decision is printed on Page 15.*

By LUTHER A. HUSTON
Special to The New York Times.

WASHINGTON, May 17—The Supreme Court unanimously outlawed today racial segregation in public schools.

Chief Justice Earl Warren read two opinions that put the stamp of unconstitutionality on school systems in twenty-one states and the District of Columbia where segregation is permissive or mandatory.

The court, taking cognizance of the problems involved in the integration of the school systems concerned, put over until the next term, beginning in October, the formulation of decrees to effectuate its 9-to-0 decision.

The opinions set aside the "separate but equal" doctrine laid down by the Supreme Court in 1896.

"In the field of public education," Chief Justice Warren said, "the doctrine of 'separate but equal' has no place. Separate educational facilities are inherently unequal."

He stated the question and supplied the answer as follows:

"We come then to the question presented: Does segregation of children in public schools solely on the basis of race, even though physical facilities and other 'tangible' factors may be equal, deprive the children of the minority group of equal educational opportunities? We believe that it does."

## ANALYZING IMAGES

Many primary sources are **images**. Images are pictures such as photographs or paintings. Historians analyze an image the same way they analyze text. They identify its context, where it came from, and what they see. They read the caption. They relate that information to what they see in the picture. They make **inferences** about the time and place, based on this information. Then they search for other evidence about the same event.

There are many images from the civil rights era. Analyze them carefully to understand the time, place, people, and ideas. The person making the image may have a different bias than those in the image. During the civil rights era, images were used to report things with a strong bias, such as the sign shown on the left.

## BE AN IMAGE DETECTIVE

When historians look at an image, they take time to study it. They look at the details. They read the caption. ■What type of image is it? ■Look at the people. How are they dressed? Does this help identify when the image was made? Do the clothes suggest the people are rich or poor? Can you guess

▼ This sign was placed in a front yard in Florida during 1959 to scare the people who lived there because they supported **integration**.

# DEATH
## TO ALL
# RACE MIXERS!
### Keep White Public Schools
# WHITE
#### BY
## Massive Armed Force!
### BE A
## Paul Revere!
### Rally Your Neighbors to
# ARMS -- SHOOT
## The Race-Mixing
# INVADERS!

### ANALYZE THIS

What bias does the writer of this sign have toward integration? What details support your conclusion?

▼ In 1963, police carry off a woman during a civil rights **demonstration**, in Brooklyn, New York.

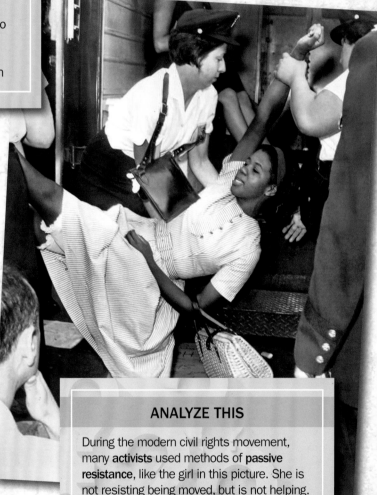

their age? Can you identify their jobs? ■Look at objects in the image. What are people holding? What other objects are in the image? Do the objects help identify what is happening or when it is happening? Look carefully at the background. Are there clues about the place, year, season, or event? Can you identify buildings, transportation, or weather?■What do you already know about the time, place, people, or event?

## ANALYZE THIS

During the modern civil rights movement, many **activists** used methods of **passive resistance**, like the girl in this picture. She is not resisting being moved, but is not helping. She is probably being taken off to jail.

"A fourth point that characterizes nonviolent resistance is a willingness to accept suffering without retaliation, to accept blows from the opponent without striking back. . . . The nonviolent resister is willing to accept violence if necessary, but never to inflict it. He does not seek to dodge jail."

Dr. Martin Luther King, Jr.

## ANALYZING MEDIA

The **mass media** played an important role in the civil rights movement. Mass media are ways of communicating (media) to reach huge numbers of people (mass). During this time, the most important media were newspapers and television.

Media that does not go out to many people is usually local. A local newspaper often reflects the values of its readers. The stories about the same civil rights event might be very different in a Selma, Alabama, newspaper compared to that in a Rutland, Vermont, newspaper. Some newspapers try to write unbiased news stories.

The civil rights movement was one of the first movements influenced by **screen media**. This is when images and words come over a screen. At the time, the main screen media was television. In some cities, people watched local news shows. These reflected a local bias. Most people watched the national news shows. Because they were national, people all over the country saw the same story. During that time, the news from the South shocked people in the rest of the country. Many did not like what they learned about how some people treated others in the South.

Today, historians can see newspapers and television stories from the civil rights era. Speeches, events, and interviews recorded at the time are primary sources.

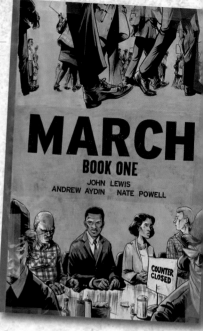

▲ In 2013, civil rights activist and congressman John Lewis published the first of three graphic history books. The books tell and show Lewis's memories of the civil rights movement and how his own ideas about civil rights and the movement grew and changed.

## ANALYZING WHAT YOU SEE AND HEAR

When historians watch a news report or video recording, they ask questions about what they see and hear. Here are some questions they might ask:

- Is this a primary source that was recorded at the time?
- What is its context? Where did the people live who made it and watched it?

- Describe what you see and/or hear. Are the people participants in the event, or are they from the media?
- What is its **perspective**, or point of view? Does it have a balanced point of view or maybe a strong bias?
- What is its purpose: to persuade, to inform, to entertain, or to explain?

▲ Television and newspaper reporters covered Malcolm X. The ideas of this African-American religious leader were different from those of other civil rights leaders. He described how African Americans should take control of their own communities instead of integrating into the white community. Unlike Dr. King, he did not believe in passive resistance.

**ANALYZE THIS**

Watch this interview in which Malcolm X talks to reporters. Go to:
www.pbslearningmedia.org/resource/iml04.soc.ush.civil.mal c1/malcolm-x-black-nationalism/
Answer some of the questions in the *Analyzing What You See and Hear* box to help you better understand the interview.

# THE CIVIL RIGHTS STORY

*"Mr. Washington . . . asks that black people give up . . . three things—First, political power; Second, insistence on civil rights; Third, higher education of Negro youth . . ."*

African-American activist W. E. B. Du Bois (1868–1963) in 1903 to counter another activist, Booker T. Washington (1856–1915)

At first, the United States allowed people to own **slaves.** Most slaves lived in the southern states. After the **Civil War** (1861–1865), the slaves were freed. At that time, many people believed that African Americans could never be as good, smart, or capable as whites. Some white racists believed this allowed them to treat them any way they wanted. This wasn't just in the South. African Americans who moved found discrimination wherever they went, even in Canada. Southern states passed **segregation** laws to keep the two races separate. Whites enforced this segregation, often with violence.

The constitution of the United States protects the rights of its people. The **Thirteenth**, **Fourteenth,** and **Fifteenth Amendments** were added to it after the Civil War. They protected the civil and voting rights of the freed slaves but were not enforced. In 1896, the Supreme Court agreed with the South's segregation. In *Plessy v. Ferguson*, it said "separate but equal" was appropriate. They ignored the fact that very little was equal between races, especially in the South.

Civil rights activists did not give up. People such as Ida B. Wells-Barnett spoke out against racial violence. Like her, many were attacked for their stand.

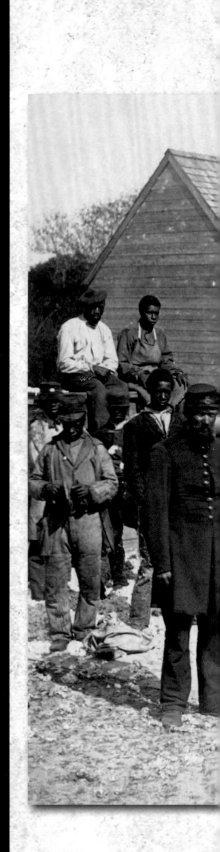

▶ These people had been slaves but were freed during the Civil War.

## JIM CROW LAWS

In the South, **Jim Crow laws** made segregation legal. They kept the races separate in almost every way. By law, African Americans sat in separate parts of theaters. They used separate water fountains. Many stores and restaurants did not allow them to enter. Most went to poor, segregated schools.

Southern whites used their political power, threats, and violence to enforce these laws. Police arrested those who broke the law, such as any African American who used the *Whites Only* bathroom. Racists often threatened or killed any African Americans who tried to vote.

Sometimes a minor event exploded into deadly violence. In 1955, 14-year-old Emmett Till became national news. He was arrested, beaten, and killed for talking to a white woman. Often, in the South, when whites killed an African American, no one was arrested. Other times, like this one, a white **jury** found white killers "not guilty."

*". . . I made up my mind that I would not give in any longer to legally imposed racial segregation and of course my arrest brought about the protests for more than a year."*

Rosa Parks

◀ Thirteen months after Rosa Parks was arrested, the United States Supreme Court said segregation on public transportation broke the Fourteenth Amendment. This reporter rode the bus with Rosa Parks the day after the decision.

## THE MONTGOMERY BUS BOYCOTT

In Montgomery, Alabama, the law said that African Americans had to sit at the back of the bus. Also, they had to give up their seat if a white person didn't have one. In 1955, Rosa Parks was arrested because she would not give up her seat.

Montgomery's African-American community decided to **protest**, or take a stand. They chose a young minister, Dr. Martin Luther King, Jr., to lead them. They **boycotted**, or stopped using, the buses. Very few had cars, so they walked everywhere. Whites threatened the walkers and burned Dr. King's home. John Lewis remembers: "Dr. King's example showed me that it was possible to do more as a minister than what I had witnessed in my own church. I was inspired." The African-American community continued to stand together. Finally, the Supreme Court said segregation on city buses was against the constitution.

This was a big step against segregation. This boycott worked because of strong **grassroots** support, strong leadership, and the Supreme Court's decision.

▲ African Americans often sang spirituals, like this one, during church. These songs came from slave songs. During the civil rights movement, they were sung in jails and during **marches**. This is the first page of the music for "Go Down, Moses," published in 1917.

## INTEGRATING SCHOOLS

Civil rights organizations formed to protect African Americans and their civil rights. They fought segregation, violence, and racism. Because of the Montgomery bus boycott, Dr. King founded the **SCLC** (Southern Christian Leadership Conference).

An older group was the **NAACP** (National Association for the Advancement of Colored People). Its lawyers, including Thurgood Marshall, worked for years to end the South's segregated schools and colleges. Most African-American schools had old books and few supplies. Their buildings needed major repairs.

In 1954, the Supreme Court decided *Brown v. Board of Education*. It said segregated schools were against the Fourteenth Amendment. The schools could not be "separate" and still be "equal." Schools had to integrate their African-American and white students.

Most schools in the South ignored the orders. Then, in 1957, nine African-American students tried to integrate the all-white high school in Little Rock, Arkansas. The governor of Arkansas stopped them. Mobs of angry whites threw bricks, beat reporters, and smashed the school. President Eisenhower sent troops

### PERSPECTIVES

In 1956, some members of Congress signed the "Southern Manifesto." It said, ". . . the [Supreme] Court . . . is destroying the amicable [friendly] relations between the white and Negro races . . . hatred and suspicion where there has been . . . friendship and understanding."

▲ In 1957, President Eisenhower sent in the military to protect nine African-American students who were integrating Little Rock Central High School.

*"I tried to see a friendly face somewhere in the mob—someone who maybe would help. I looked into the face of an old woman and it seemed a kind face, but when I looked at her again, she spat on me."*

Elizabeth Eckford, one of the nine Little Rock students

to Arkansas to enforce the federal **court** orders. Troops stayed all year to protect the students. The next year, the governor closed all the high schools. He refused to integrate them. This was the first big battle over integrating schools.

Another battle was in 1962 at The University of Mississippi. The university refused to follow a federal court order that said it had to accept James Meredith as its first African-American student. Mississippi's governor said he would never allow integration. President Kennedy sent troops to Mississippi to enforce the order and to protect Meredith.

Some historians see the Montgomery bus boycott as a turning point in the civil rights movement. Others feel it was *Brown v. Board of Education* or later actions, such as the **sit-ins**, that were the turning point. All these events changed American life, especially in the South.

## DEFINITIONS

Civil rights activists used many forms of protest to get attention:

**Boycotts:** Refusal to use or buy a product or service

**Nonviolence:** Use of peaceful means, not violence, to bring about change

**Sit-ins:** Groups of people sitting somewhere and refusing to move

**Marches:** Groups of people walking together to bring attention to an idea or action

**Demonstrations:** Large public meetings to protest against or show support for something

**Protests:** Demonstrations or events where people show strong feelings against something

◀ The Ku Klux Klan (KKK) is a racist group. It threatened, attacked, and murdered African Americans. Its members sometimes used burning crosses.

## ANALYZE THIS

How does this photograph make you feel? How would you feel if this happened in front of your house?

## NONVIOLENT PROTESTS

By 1960, little had changed in the South. Most African Americans could not vote in southern states. They did not go to integrated schools. Federal civil rights laws and court decisions were not enforced.

In the early 1960s, civil rights activists tried some new actions. Most still used nonviolent methods. In Greensboro, North Carolina, African-American college students returned to a store's lunch counter every day for weeks. Each day, they refused to leave until they were served. Since they were not white, they were not served. This was the civil rights movement's first important sit-in. Sit-ins spread quickly.

College students formed their own civil rights organization, the Student Nonviolent Coordinating Committee or **SNCC**. They did many things to change segregated life, but not always in the way older leaders wanted.

In 1961, another national civil rights group, **CORE** (the Congress of Racial Equality), took action. Thirteen white and black **volunteers** got on a bus. These Freedom Riders sat together as they

▼ In 1960, John F. Kennedy ran for president. African Americans supported him because he supported civil rights. During his campaign he called Dr. King, who was in jail. Kennedy's brother, Robert, helped to get King released.

"*If they can stop us with violence the movement is dead.*"

Diane Nash, a Freedom Rider and SNCC founder

### EVIDENCE RECORD CARD

Kennedy for President campaign brochure showing him with civil rights leaders
**LEVEL** Primary source
**MATERIAL** Campaign brochure
**LOCATION** Probably for distribution in African-American neighborhoods
**DATE** 1960
**SOURCE** Getty Images

rode across the South on a bus. They went into segregated bus stations together. They remained nonviolent. Their bus was surrounded by angry white mobs. They were arrested, beaten, and their bus was firebombed. More Freedom Riders took the place of those hurt or arrested. The local police did not protect them, so the president sent protection.

In spring 1963, civil rights leaders in Birmingham, Alabama, held a protest march. Hundreds of African-American children walked in it. The police chief ordered his men to use police dogs and fire hoses against the children. Almost 1,000 people were arrested. The television and newspaper pictures shocked people everywhere. Once again, they saw that segregation, violent white **resistance**, and racial injustice remained major problems in the South.

## PERSPECTIVES

In 1961, CBS news interviewed people in Birmingham, Alabama. Listen to how a white woman and a black civil rights activist feel about what is happening in their city: www.paleycenter.org/cbs-reports-who-speaks-for-birmingham

## ANALYZE THIS

How would you describe the men sitting at the counter? Who are the other people in this picture? What are the men wearing or holding that helps identify their jobs?

▲ This integrated group of Freedom Riders was arrested when they tried to buy lunch at this bus station.

## THE MARCH ON WASHINGTON

In June 1963, President Kennedy sent troops in to help integrate The University of Alabama. Afterward, he told Americans that they needed a stronger civil rights law. His speech gave many African Americans hope. However, a few hours later, the civil rights leader Medgar Evers was murdered.

Soon after, the leaders of six national civil rights groups met. They worked together to plan a demonstration to support a civil rights bill. It was called "The March on Washington for Jobs and Freedom." No one knew how many people would come. Many were afraid there would be riots.

On August 28, 1963, bus after bus arrived in Washington, D.C. People traveled for hours from all over. Most were African American, but thousands of whites came, too. Hundreds of reporters were there. Much of the march was on television. It was the biggest demonstration ever held in the United States. And it was peaceful.

▶ More than 250,000 people came to Washington, D.C., for The March on Washington for Jobs and Freedom.

*"It ought to be possible . . . for every American to enjoy the privileges of being American without regard to his race or his color."*

President Kennedy, in a televised speech about the need for a civil rights act, June 11, 1963

### ANALYZE THIS

Historians look at many sources about the same event. Compare all the primary and secondary sources in this book on The March on Washington. Analyze each carefully. How does each add something different to what you know about the march?

People filled the streets. They marched to the Lincoln Memorial. There was singing and praying and speeches. Important civil rights leaders spoke. Later, the leaders met with the president. Everyone else peacefully returned home.

A few weeks later, four young African-American girls died when a church in Birmingham, Alabama, was bombed. On November 22, President Kennedy was shot. His successor, President Johnson, continued Kennedy's promise to pass the Civil Rights Bill. Congress argued for over 80 days. Finally, the bill passed.

President Johnson signed the Civil Rights Act of 1964 with Dr. King nearby. It was the most important civil rights law in United States history. It made discrimination illegal in public places such as restaurants, theaters, and hotels. Schools had to be integrated. It improved voter registration. It also gave the federal government ways to enforce civil rights laws.

### ANALYZE THIS

The most famous speech at The March on Washington was Dr. King's "I Have a Dream" speech. Hear it at: http://mlk-kpp01.stanford.edu/index.php/encyclopedia/documentsentry/doc_august_28_1963_i_have_a_dream/ Listen closely to what he is saying and how he is saying it. How did people react to his rhythms and words?

▲ Singer Mahalia Jackson was one of many famous actors, singers, and civil rights leaders who sang or spoke at The March on Washington.

▲ During 1964's Freedom Summer, civil rights volunteers helped Mississippi's African Americans get ready to register to vote.

## FREEDOM SUMMER

The summer of 1964 was called Freedom Summer. CORE and SNCC trained more than 700 white college students. They moved to rural Mississippi. They wanted to help African Americans **register** to vote. The volunteers were warned that racists would treat them badly in the South. Southern newspapers warned that an invasion was coming from the North.

In 1962, only 6.7 percent of Mississippi's African Americans could vote. This was the lowest percentage in the country. Local officials refused to let these people register to vote. In some places, a test was given. African Americans were asked very hard questions. Whites were asked easy ones. Sometimes African Americans who tried to register were beaten or fired from their job.

Early in Freedom Summer, three volunteers disappeared. Two months later, their bodies were found. The mass media widely reported these events. Mark and Betty Levy were Freedom Summer volunteers. They wrote: "The murder of our three co-workers brought home to all of us the reality of the organized and state-supported violence that is pervasive [widespread]. We also realize that if two of the three men had not been white Northerners the incident would never have received such vast publicity."

The volunteers were scared, but they stayed. They lived with African-American families. They taught in "Freedom Schools." Some taught reading and writing. Others taught how to fill out forms

"The freedom schools were the most impressive part of the program. . . . The oldest student was an 85-year-old man who had taught himself to read, but wanted to learn more in order to take the registration test . . ."

Terri Shaw, civil rights worker

and pass the test. Life wasn't easy. Volunteers and families were **harassed**, beaten, and arrested. Churches and homes were bombed. That summer in Mississippi, 17,000 African Americans tried to register. Only 1,600 became voters. But African Americans were proud of their new strength. They even started a new political party, the Mississippi Freedom Democratic Party.

Later that year, Dr. King received the Nobel Peace Prize. He was the youngest man to receive it and only the second African American.

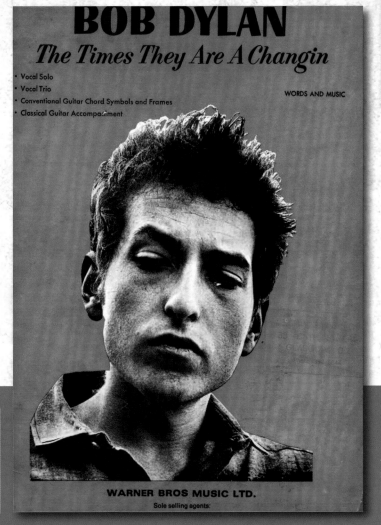

WARNER BROS MUSIC LTD.
Sole selling agents:

## PERSPECTIVES

What points of view do Mark and Betty Levy write about during Freedom Summer?

"The woman who we are living with has been threatened with loss of her job because she is housing us. Yet, she says with pride, she'll go back to the fields and pick cotton if she has to, rather than give in."

◀ Bob Dylan's song "The Times They Are A-Changin'" captured the spirit of change in the United States.

### SELMA TO MONTGOMERY

The Civil Rights Act of 1964 passed. It changed little for African Americans who wanted to vote. That didn't stop civil rights groups. In 1965, the SNCC, SCLC, and other groups went to Alabama. They went with African Americans to register to vote in Selma. Many, including Dr. King, were arrested. Others waited five hours to take a test but were still not allowed to become voters.

March 7 was the first "Selma to Montgomery" march. About 600 people peacefully marched through Selma, until lawmen blocked their way. They told the marchers to leave, then attacked them with clubs and tear gas. That day is called "Bloody Sunday." That night, television shows were interrupted by the news from Selma.

Two days later, Dr. King led a second march. Religious leaders came from all over the country. About 2,000 people marched. Then they stopped, got on their knees, and prayed. Then they stood up and returned home.

During that time, talks were going on between the president, the governor, and the march's leaders. Since the governor

▲ On Bloody Sunday, police used clubs and tear gas to break up a peaceful march for voting rights in Selma, Alabama.

### ANALYZE THIS

Where and when did the events in each of these pictures take place? How did the events of one photograph cause the events in the second?

would not protect them, President Johnson sent protection for a third march. Those marchers left Selma on March 21. They walked more than 50 miles to the state capital of Montgomery. Some days, only a few hundred marched. On the seventh day, more than 25,000 marchers entered the capital. Everything seemed peaceful, until a volunteer was shot and killed by KKK members. National and international news programs covered all these events. They showed how determined African Americans were to get their rights.

That summer, Congress passed the Voting Rights Act and President Johnson signed it. States such as Mississippi and Alabama had to register eligible African Americans. The number of African-American voters in the South suddenly skyrocketed. Within a year, about 450,000 were registered to vote.

## PERSPECTIVES

In March 1965, after Bloody Sunday, the marchers went to the courts to get protection. John Lewis, a march leader, answered questions in court:

*Question:* "Did you see any of the marchers use any violence at all in an effort to defend themselves or to fight the police officers?"

*Answer by John Lewis:* "There was no act of violence or any type of retaliation [payback] . . . on the part of any of the demonstrators."

▲ Two days after Bloody Sunday in Alabama, a march in New York City showed support for the Selma marchers.

## THE CHANGING MOVEMENT

The civil rights movement began to split. Some African Americans felt things were not changing fast enough. They stopped supporting nonviolence and integration. They listened to different leaders. SNCC leader Stokely Carmichael talked about "Black Power." He wanted African Americans to take charge of their neighborhoods. He wanted them to take pride in being black.

One religious group, the **Nation of Islam**, wanted African Americans to stay separate from whites. Its most powerful speaker, Malcolm X, spoke against nonviolence. He felt the nonviolence movement was not doing enough. See the link on page 17 to hear his ideas. Then a few months after he formed his own group, he was killed. Other groups took up his ideas.

The Black Panthers talked about killing white police. They also started education, health, and economic programs for **urban** African Americans. They were a small group, but frightened many whites. The **FBI**—a government agency—kept going after them.

### ANALYZE THIS

Compare the visual and written primary sources on these pages. How do their details support this statement from a secondary source: "The Panthers' platform attracted many young African Americans, while their public embrace of violence frightened many whites."

"The voice of the [Black] Panthers . . . is increasingly the voice of young ghetto blacks who in city after city this summer have been confronting cops with bricks, bottles, and bullets."

Sol Stern, journalist, 1967

▲ The Black Panthers often appeared with weapons. They did not follow Dr. King's ideas of nonviolence.

## URBAN RIOTS

Urban African Americans outside the South often faced widespread segregation. It was not the law, but it existed. They lived in segregated urban neighborhoods. Their schools were not very good and there were few good jobs available nearby. Apartments and houses were falling apart. Sometimes, whites refused to sell them houses in better neighborhoods.

Every summer from 1964 to 1968, angry, urban African Americans rioted. In 1967, there were riots in 127 cities all over the country. Rioters threw rocks and bottles of gasoline. They turned over cars and **looted** stores. Many people were killed. Neighborhood buildings and businesses were destroyed. A 1968 report warned that people were frustrated and angry. It recommended many changes. Few happened.

### EVIDENCE RECORD CARD

Photograph of Detroit neighborhood after four nights of riots
LEVEL  Primary source
MATERIAL  Black-and-white photograph
LOCATION  Detroit, Michigan
DATE  July 27, 1967
SOURCE  Topfoto

▲ During an urban riot in Detroit, African Americans destroyed much of this inner-city neighborhood.

## THE LOSS OF A LEADER

Dr. King continued to be an important world leader. He worked on many important issues that affected African Americans. He spoke about education, war, poverty, and jobs. He continued to use nonviolent methods.

Then, in 1968, he was assassinated. The civil rights movement lost its most important leader. He was not forgotten. He is honored in many ways because what he did and how he did it changed the country and influenced the world.

## SCHOOL BUSING

Civil rights activists wanted to integrate schools, but not just in the South. Even outside the South, city schools in poor African-Americans neighborhoods had few white students. In the 1970s, federal courts ordered urban schools to move students around by bus. They wanted schools to have a better racial balance.

Many parents did not like school **busing** and fought it. They wanted their children to go to local schools. They didn't like their children riding the bus

▲ The Lorraine Motel in Memphis, Tennessee, where Dr. King was shot, is now part of a civil rights museum.

▲ The memorial to Dr. Martin Luther King, Jr. is in Washington, D.C. It includes a line from his "I Have a Dream" speech.

*"If the Civil Rights Movement is 'dead,' and if it gave us nothing else, it gave us each other forever. It gave some of us bread, some of us shelter, some of us knowledge and pride, all of us comfort. . . . It broke the pattern of black servitude in this country. . . . It gave us history and men far greater than Presidents. It gave us heroes, selfless men of courage and strength, for our little boys and girls to follow. It gave us hope for tomorrow. It called us to life."*

Alice Walker, African-American author, 1967

for a long time each day. They didn't want their children to go to schools in poor neighborhoods. Those schools were often not as good as schools in the white neighborhoods. Many parents fought busing. Some white families left the city. Some put their children in private schools. Yet, many inner-city students got a better education. More African-American students graduated. More went to college and got good jobs.

Phyllis Ellison was an African-American student in Boston. She was bused to a white school. She said, ". . . for the civil rights part of it, I would do it over, because I felt like my rights were being violated by the white people of South Boston telling me that I could not go to South Boston High School. . . ."

The Supreme Court has changed its stand on school busing. Today it accepts local schools. It has left many urban schools even more segregated than before 1954. The poor schools still do not have enough money for books, computers, or building repairs. They still have trouble providing a good education.

## PERSPECTIVES

This 2013 story compiles primary evidence about school busing in Charlotte, North Carolina, during the late 1960s and early 1970s. Follow the link to: http://retroreport.org/the-battle-for-busing/

What different attitudes do the people in this news report have about busing in the Charlotte, North Carolina, schools?

◀ These parents blame the Supreme Court for ordering school busing.

# OBAMA
## RACIAL BARRIER FALLS IN DECISIVE VICTORY

Democrats in Congress
Strengthen Grip

President-elect Barack Obama with his wife, Michelle, and their daughters in Chicago on Tuesday night.

THE CHALLENGE
No Time for Laurels;
Now the Hard Part
By PETER BAKER

THE MOMENT
After Decades,
A Time to Reap
By KEVIN SACK

THE PROMISE
For Many Abroad,
An Ideal Renewed
By ETHAN BRONNER

**EVIDENCE RECORD CARD**

*The New York Times* front page
**LEVEL** Primary source
**MATERIAL** Newspaper
**LOCATION** New York City, New York
**DATE** November 5, 2008
**SOURCE** Image Works

## THE END OF AN ERA

The civil rights era slowly ended in the 1970s. The movement met some of its goals. There is greater equality for African Americans in the South. Jim Crow laws can no longer be used to enforce segregation. Graduation rates of students climbed from 23 percent in 1962 to 86 percent in 2012. With a better education and better jobs, more African Americans moved into the middle class. Many more moved out of poor neighborhoods or worked to improve them.

In 1967, NAACP lawyer Thurgood Marshall was appointed to the United States Supreme Court. Other civil rights leaders, such as John Lewis, went into politics to continue the fight. In 2014, Lewis is one of 44 African-American members of Congress. When Barack Obama ran for president in 2008, Americans' prejudice and faith were both exposed. When he won, he became the country's first African-American president. These examples encourage other African Americans. Today, African

◀ On November 4, 2008, American voters elected Barack Obama to be president of the United States. He became the country's first African-American president. He was reelected in 2012.

*"The temptation, coming home, is to say that nothing has changed. . . . Yet it has changed . . . . profoundly in the decade since the sit-ins and the Freedom Rides. . . . Black people are still poor and still imprisoned by their poverty. But they go places they never have been before— the 'white' and the 'colored' signs have come down almost everywhere . . ."*

Karl Fleming, civil rights journalist

◀ Over the years, Americans have honored the people of the civil rights movement in many ways. These stamps honor those that were part of it and its outcome.

▼ High school students, after desegregation, stand in line in a cafeteria.

Americans in the South can vote. Many are elected to city and state offices.

The civil rights movement didn't solve everything. It didn't end racism. It didn't cure poverty. It didn't improve urban schools. There are still not enough good jobs, especially in the inner city. Cultural problems, such as drugs and gang violence, have grown. The deaths of African-American young men often reveal white fears and too-quick responses by police. These are still problems to be solved.

During the civil rights era, thousands of people risked their lives. Many died in the fight for civil rights. Most did it because they wanted to make the United States a better place. They succeeded.

*"To dismiss the magnitude of this progress—to suggest, as some sometimes do, that little has changed—that dishonors the courage and the sacrifice of those who paid the price to march in those years."*

President Barack Obama, August 2013

# HISTORY REPEATED

*"Because they marched, America became more free and more fair–not just for African Americans, but for women and Latinos, Asians and Native Americans; for Catholics, Jews, and Muslims; for gays, for Americans with disabilities. America changed for you and for me."*

President Barack Obama, 2013

Because of the civil rights movement, other groups demanded rights. They copied its nonviolent marches, grassroots volunteers, and court cases. Women, Native Americans, and Latinos formed groups. They worked to gain more rights, more media coverage, and new laws.

Some women had worked in the civil rights movement. Later, they became part of the women's rights movement. Women wanted legal, health, and economic rights. They wanted to be able to get their own credit card or mortgage. They developed grassroots support, and encouraged women to be more active in politics. New jobs opened to women. Today, more women serve in the military, are scientists, or become advisors to presidents.

Other groups, such as Native Americans, Latinos, and the LGBT community, also took lessons from the civil rights movement. Most used nonviolent methods. They held marches and boycotts. They used political pressure and went to court.

Each group keeps trying to improve life in the United States. They learn from the past to make sure that, in the future, all people will have the rights that the constitution promises them.

The American civil rights movement inspired changes in Canada, too. Black Canadians worked to end discrimination. Other groups worked to improve the political rights of people in Quebec and for Native people.

▼ Elizabeth Holtzman (second from right) was one of many powerful women at this 1992 march for women's rights.

## PERSPECTIVES

People read history for the stories. The stories of the civil rights movement show how people can be treated unfairly by a government or by other people. Yet the stories inspire us because people came together to create change. The government stepped in to protect people. And people made a difference by taking action.

## WORLDWIDE RIGHTS

People all over the world watched the civil rights movement as it took action in the United States. Today, many who do not have many rights in their own country study the movement.

In South Africa, the government enforced **apartheid** laws. These, like the Jim Crow laws, kept black Africans segregated from whites. Many people fought and died trying to end this discrimination. They used both violent and nonviolent methods. After the civil rights era, many Americans saw the injustice in apartheid. They held protests against apartheid. They pushed the government and businesses to stop doing business in South Africa.

▶ In South Africa, apartheid laws segregated people by race. These people are protesting by sitting in railroad cars reserved for Europeans or whites.

SLEGS BLANKES.
EUROPEANS ONLY.

### ANALYZE THIS

Compare the nonviolent methods shown in these two photographs. What are the differences and what are the similarities?

"We are . . . conscious that here in the southern part of the country, you have experienced the degradation of racial segregation. . . . Let us all acclaim now, 'Let freedom ring in South Africa. Let freedom ring wherever the people's rights are trampled upon.' "

The future president of South Africa, Nelson Mandela, speaking in 1990

Eventually, South Africa's government changed the laws. One anti-apartheid leader, Nelson Mandela, was released from prison in 1990. Soon after, he was elected president of South Africa. His election was possible because many black Africans were finally able to vote.

In 1989, the Chinese Government reacted to demonstrations. Protestors wanted more economic freedom and a bigger say in the government. The government sent in tanks to end the demonstration. Hundreds were killed. Thousands were wounded. Thousands more were arrested.

Events such as these are not unique in today's world. People are fighting for their civil rights in Russia, France, Egypt, and India. Their demands include that their government give them more political and economic control. They want to end laws segregating one race or religion. Many look at America's civil rights movement for ideas, methods, and inspiration.

None of it is finished. The world's people, everywhere, continue to fight for their human and civil rights.

▼ In 1989, thousands of people protested in Tiananmen Square in Beijing, China. They wanted individual rights and more democratic freedom.

# TIMELINE

**1860**

**1861** Civil War begins

**1863** Emancipation Proclamation frees slaves in southern states

**1865** Civil War ends; Thirteenth Amendment abolishes slavery in the United States

**1868** Fourteenth Amendment forbids states from denying any person specific civil rights

**1870** Fifteenth Amendment grants men the right to vote regardless of race, color, or former slavery

**1896** *Plessy v. Ferguson*: the U.S. Supreme Court approves "separate but equal" segregation and Jim Crow laws in southern states

**1900**

**1917** Harlem Renaissance begins

**1948** President Truman integrates the military

**1950**

**1954** U.S. Supreme Court decides *Brown v. Board of Education* requiring schools to integrate; modern civil rights era begins

**1955 August:** Emmett Till is murdered **December:** Rosa Parks is arrested and the Montgomery bus boycott begins

**1956** U.S. Supreme Court decides segregation on public buses is illegal; Montgomery bus boycott ends

**1957** Southern Christian Leadership Conference (SCLC) founded; Little Rock Central High School integrated after President Eisenhower sends in federal troops to protect students

**1960**

**1960** College students conduct sit-ins to integrate places to eat; John F. Kennedy is elected president with strong African-American support

**1961** Freedom Riders are attacked and jailed as they integrate public transportation; President Kennedy orders federal protection

**1962** Federal troops protect James Meredith, The University of Mississippi's first African-American student

**1963 May:** Birmingham, Alabama, police use fire hoses and dogs on peaceful demonstrators; thousands are jailed **June:** President Kennedy announces the need for a civil rights bill; the same night activist Medgar Evers is murdered **August 28:** 250,000 attend The March on Washington for Jobs and Freedom and hear Dr. King's "I Have a Dream" speech **September:** Church bomb kills four young girls in Birmingham, Alabama **November 22:** President Kennedy is assassinated; President Johnson takes office

**1964** Freedom Summer: Volunteers get African Americans ready to register to vote; three civil rights workers are murdered; riots in Harlem, Detroit, and other cities; Civil Rights Act is passed; Dr. Martin Luther King, Jr. receives Nobel Peace Prize

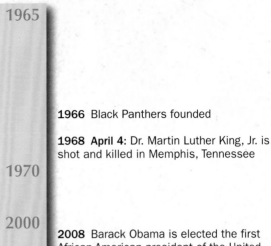

**1965 February 21**: Malcolm X is murdered
**March 7**: Bloody Sunday: Selma to Montgomery march is stopped by police
**March 21–28**: Selma to Montgomery march resumes with federal protection
**August**: Voting Rights Act enforces Fifteenth Amendment
**August 11–17**: Watts riots in Los Angeles

**1967** Urban riots break out in 127 cities; Thurgood Marshall becomes first African American on the U.S. Supreme Court

**1971** U.S. Supreme Court requires schools all over the country to integrate by busing students

**2013 August 28**: Celebration held for 50th Anniversary of The March on Washington

1965

1970

2000

**1966** Black Panthers founded

**1968 April 4**: Dr. Martin Luther King, Jr. is shot and killed in Memphis, Tennessee

**2008** Barack Obama is elected the first African-American president of the United States

**Segregation in Schools before Brown v Board of Education, 1954**

Required
No Legislation
Optional/Limited
Forbidden

500 miles
500 km

# BIBLIOGRAPHY

## QUOTATIONS

p.4: Dr. Martin Luther King, Jr. quote: *Strength to Love*. Harper & Row, 1963. Page 10.

p.6: Ross Barnett quote: http://microsites.jfklibrary.org/olemiss/controversy/ Speech broadcast on September 13, 1962.

p.8: Nan Grogan Orrock quote: Bass, Patrick Henry. *Like a Mighty Stream: The March on Washington, August 28, 1963*. Running Press, 2002. Page 143.

p.11: Badger, Anthony J. *Different Perspectives on the Civil Rights Movement*. www.gilderlehrman.org/history-by-era/civil-rights-movement/essays/different-perspectives-civil-rights-movement

p.11: Rubin, Susan Goldman. *Freedom Summer: The 1964 Struggle for Civil Rights in Mississippi*. Holiday House, 2014. Page 7.

Branch, Taylor. *Parting the Waters: America in the King Years 1954–63*. Simon & Schuster, 1998.

p.12: United States Supreme Court, *Brown v. Board of Education*, 1954: www.ourdocuments.gov/doc.php?flash=true&doc=87

p.15: Dr. Martin Luther King, Jr. quote: *Stride Toward Freedom: The Montgomery Story*. Harper & Brothers, 1958; in *The Civil Rights Movement*. Jill Karson, ed. Greenhaven Press, 2005.

p.18: W. E. B. Du Bois quote: *The Souls of Black Folk*. A.C. McClurg & Co, 1903. http://xroads.virginia.edu/~HYPER/DUBOIS/ch03.html

p.20: Rosa Parks quote: Interview by the Academy of Achievement. June 2, 1995. www.digitalhistory.uh.edu/disp_textbook.cfm?smtid=3&psid=1142

p.22: The Southern Manifesto: http://history.house.gov/Historical-Highlights/1951-2000/The-Southern-Manifesto-of-1956/

p.22: Elizabeth Eckford quote: www.encyclopediaofarkansas.net/encyclopedia/entry-detail.aspx?entryID=723

p.24: Diane Nash quote: www.gilderlehrman.org/history-by-era/civil-rights-movement/essays/civil-rights-movement

p.26: John F. Kennedy quote: www.jfklibrary.org/Asset-Viewer/LH8F_0Mzv0e6Ro1yEm74Ng.aspx

p.28: Terri Shaw quote: www.pbs.org/wgbh/amex/eyesontheprize/sources/ps_summer.html

pp.28, 29: *Levy, Mark and Betty. "A Letter From Mississippi." Long Island Press*, Sunday, July 19, 1964. http://digital.lib.miamioh.edu/cdm/compoundobject/collection/fstxt/id/1624/rec/5

p.31: John Lewis testimony: www.archives.gov/exhibits/eyewitness/html.php?section=2

p.32: Norton, Mary Beth; Sheriff, Carol; et. al. *A People and A Nation: A History of the United States*. 9th edition. Boston: Wadsworth, Cengage Learning, 2012. Page 845.

p.32: Sol Stern quote: "Call of the Black Panthers." *The New York Times* magazine, August 6, 1967; in *Reporting Civil Rights, Part Two, American Journalism 1963–1973*. The Library of America, 2003.

p.34: Dr. Martin Luther King, Jr. quote on monument: www.nps.gov/media/photo/gallery.htm?id=313AF650-1DD8-B71C-07476509DBD56534

p.34: Alice Walker quote: "The Civil Rights Movement, What Good Was It?" *American Scholar* 36 (Autumn 1967); in Finkenbine, Roy E. *Sources of the African-American Past*. Longman, 1997.

p.35: Phyllis Ellison quote: "Being Bused." Hampton, Henry, and Steve Fayer. *Voices of Freedom: An Oral History of the Civil Rights Movement from the 1950s through the 1980s*. Bantam Books, 1990. www.pbs.org/wgbh/amex/eyesontheprize/reflect/r11_bused.html

p.36: Karl Fleming quote: "The South Revisited After a Momentous Decade." *Newsweek*, August 10, 1970; in *Reporting Civil Rights, Part Two, American Journalism 1963–1973*. The Library of America, 2003.

pp.37, 38: Barack Obama quotes: www.whitehouse.gov/photos-and-video/video/2013/08/28/president-obama-marks-50th-anniversary-march-washington#transcript

p.40: Nelson Mandela quote: *The Atlanta Journal–Constitution*, June 28, 1990. www.ajc.com/news/news/national/nelson-mandela-1990-visit-atlanta-king-center/nYXk3/

# INTERNET GUIDELINES

Finding good source material on the Internet can sometimes be a challenge.
Analyze each site you find and check out the information on it. How reliable is it?

- Who writes and/or sponsors the page? Is it an expert in the field, a person who experienced the event, or just a person with a strong opinion?
- Is the site well known and up to date? Government and college websites often have lots of easy-to-find sources and information.
- Can you verify the facts with another source? Always double-check information by comparing the information on several websites.

- Did you determine whether what you find is a primary or secondary source? Do your secondary sources seem to be based on a variety of primary sources?
- Have you kept a list of the websites you've visited? This can help you verify information later.

## TO FIND OUT MORE

### Non-Fiction

Freedman, Russell. *Freedom Walkers: The Story of the Montgomery Bus Boycott.* Holiday House, 2009.

Kanefield, Teri. *The Girl from the Tar Paper School: Barbara Rose Johns and the Advent of the Civil Rights Movement.* Abrams, 2014.

Levinson, Cynthia Y. *We've Got a Job: The 1963 Birmingham Children's March.* Peachtree Publishers, 2012.

Lewis, John, Andrew Aydin, and Nate Powell. *MARCH: Books One and Two.* Top Shelf Productions, 2013, 2015.

Pinkney, Andrea Davis. *Let It Shine: Stories of Black Women Freedom Fighters.* HMH Books for Young Readers, 2013.

Rubin, Susan Goldman. *Freedom Summer: The 1964 Struggle for Civil Rights in Mississippi.* Holiday House, 2014.

Turck, Mary C. *The Civil Rights Movement for Kids: A History with 21 Activities.* Chicago Review Press, 2000.

### Fiction

Abbott, Tony. *Lunch-Box Dream.* Farrar, Straus and Giroux, 2011.

Curtis, Christopher Paul. *The Watsons Go to Birmingham—1963.* Delacourt Books for Young Readers, 1995.

Scattergood, Augusta. *Glory Be.* Scholastic Press, 2012.

Wiles, Deborah. *Freedom Summer.* Atheneum Books for Young Readers. 2001.

Williams-Garcia, Rita. *One Crazy Summer.* Amistad, 2010.

## WEBSITES AND MULTIMEDIA

Many websites carry the speeches and news footage from the civil rights era. Some include primary text, image, and audio-visual sources.

The Library of Congress has several exhibits on civil rights. One is about Jackie Robinson, the first African American in modern Major League Baseball. Another compiles many "Voices of Civil Rights." African American Odyssey includes chapters on the Civil Rights Era.
http://memory.loc.gov/ammem/aaohtml/exhibit/aopart9.html

The PBS series American Experience has a website with extensive materials for its "Eyes on the Prize" series, including interviews, timelines, and primary sources.
www.pbs.org/wgbh/amex/eyesontheprize/

The Southern Poverty Law Center's Teaching Tolerance project has an activity book on the Civil Rights Movement. www.tolerance.org/civil-rights-activity-book

The Civil Rights Movement Veterans Website offers many materials, articles, interviews, and primary sources. www.crmvet.org/about1.htm

Several presidential libraries have websites with primary sources about civil rights. www.jfklibrary. org/JFK/JFK-in-History/Civil-Rights-Movement.aspx

President Johnson's Presidential Library has a civil rights website for kids.
www.lbjlib.utexas.edu/johnson/lbjforkids/civil.shtm

The Martin Luther King, Jr. Research and Education Institute at Stanford University has an extensive website.
It includes a detailed encyclopedia of the civil rights movement, primary sources, and Dr. King's speeches.
https://kinginstitute.stanford.edu/liberation-curriculum/classroom-resources

# GLOSSARY

**activist** A person who is actively working toward social or political change

**African American** A person in the United States with dark skin whose ancestors came from Africa

**analyze** To study closely and determine how the evidence fits together

**apartheid** A system used in South Africa based on the segregation of the races

**bias** An opinion that is in favor of or against something or someone

**bill** A proposed law going through a legislature where it is discussed until it is voted on to decide whether it will become law

**black** A common term used for people with dark skin

**boycott** To stop using or refusing to buy something

**busing** The moving of students around by bus to better balance racial integration in schools

**century** A period of 100 years

**chronological** The order in which events happened

**civil rights** The rights and protections the government promises all people

**civil rights movement** Action from about 1954 to 1971 involving demonstrations to obtain equal civil rights for African Americans

**Civil War** War fought from 1861–1865 between the Confederacy (southern states) and the Union (the rest of the states)

**colored** A term no longer used for people who have dark skin

**Congress** The legislative branch of the U.S. Government, including the House of Representatives and the Senate

**constitution** Written laws and principles by which a country is governed

**context** Everything about a time and place

**CORE** Congress of Racial Equality; a civil rights group founded in 1942

**court** A place where a judge and/or jury hears cases to determine if laws are being followed

**decade** A period of 10 years

**demonstration** A large public meeting to protest against or show support for something

**discriminate** To treat with less favor than someone else

**discrimination** When people's rights are interfered with because they are different in some way—often their race

**document** An official paper containing evidence

**era** A period during which something, an event, or a person is very important

**evidence** Facts to prove something, such as what happened at an event

**FBI** Federal Bureau of Investigation—it spied on and was aggressive toward many civil rights leaders

**federal** Something that is part of the U.S. Government and is not under the control of a state or city

**Fifteenth Amendment** Constitutional change granting men who are U.S. citizens the right to vote, without regard to color or having been a slave

**Fourteenth Amendment** Constitutional change granting citizenship to all persons born in the United States, forbidding the states from taking away the civil rights of these people

**generation** Refers to a group of people who were born at about the same time

**grassroots** Everyday people working at a local level toward a goal

**harass** To give unwanted and uninvited physical or verbal contact that is usually part of an unpleasant situation

**historian** A person who uses evidence to determine what happened in the past

**history** What happened in the past based on evidence

**images** Visual sources such as photos and paintings

**inference** Something that is suggested or implied

**injustice** Unfairness or the violation of a person's rights

**integration** Combining two or more groups as equals

**Jim Crow laws** Laws passed in southern states at the end of the 19th century that enforced the segregation of African Americans

**jury** Group of people in a court who listen to a case, then decide whether someone is guilty

**loot** To steal, often during a riot

**march** A walk with many people to bring attention to a cause

**mass media** Methods of communications (media) that reach huge numbers of people (mass), including radio and television

**movement** A series of organized events to reach a specific goal

**NAACP** National Association for the Advancement of Colored People; a civil rights group founded in 1909

**national** Having to do with the federal government, not the state governments

**Nation of Islam** African-American organization that combined Islam with black nationalism

**negro** Term used for African Americans until the late 1960s; now thought rude

**nonviolence** The principle of not using violence to achieve one's goals

**passive resistance** A nonviolent method whereby a person resists something by not cooperating

**perspective** Point of view or attitude toward something

**prejudice** Strong, often unfair, opinions

**primary sources** Documents, images, or items that were created or used by someone who was at a specific time and place

**protest** An event where people show their strong feelings against something

**race** A group of people with the same language, history, and culture

**racism** Prejudice based on the belief that one race is better than another

**register** To enroll to do something, such as vote

**resistance** Opposition to a people or organization

**riot** A public disturbance by a large crowd

**SCLC** Southern Christian Leadership Conference; founded in 1957 by Martin Luther King, Jr. and others

**screen media** When images and words come over a screen, such as a television

**secondary source** Something that draws evidence from primary sources

**segregation** Separating races through inferior treatment

**sit-in** Nonviolent protest of sitting and refusing to move

**slave** A person owned by another and treated as property, without any rights

**SNCC** Student Nonviolent Coordinating Committee; an organization founded in 1960 to protest racism

**source** A place to get information

**Supreme Court** Highest court in the United States

**text source** Something with words from which someone can get information

**Thirteenth Amendment** Constitutional amendment that abolished slavery throughout the U.S.

**urban** Having to do with something in a city

**volunteer** A person who offers to take part in something

# INDEX